Stephen the Phlebc

Nadia Lines

Published by Nine Pens

2022

www.ninepens.co.uk

ISBN: 978-1-7398274-5-8

011

This book is dedicated to the people within it

Epithalamion

We were married in *Claire's Accessories*.
Two Best-Friend crown rings, two lattes,
the cashier utterly baffled at being asked to perform the ceremony.

The way you look on King's Parade –
your Camus curled open, your dyed fringe
glistening, black coat, army boots, an earnest beret…

How can I not feel that twinge
of envy? When you were smaller,
you were a horse girl. Your septum piercing cringes.

But I liked *Malory Towers*, too. Let me pour
you a midnight feast – scones, jam, cream,
the Spanish hot chocolate you adore.

I see us in pinafores, sitting by the sea.
I see us as we are – spilling ourselves, girlish, girly.

To the Chaplain

A Golden Shovel after John 3:16

'Yes, the weather is lovely. Now, what are you really here for?'
you asked. 'Help. I had always been hollow, but somehow, last April: God.'
We watched a woman fishing, a heron skimming. 'I can't stop thinking of His
        ribs, I am so

scared.' You said 'Let me tell you a secret that preachers forget. Jesus loved
food. He ordered bread for girls just risen from the dead. He saw the
Kingdom of Heaven in olives and tangerines. To Him the world

just needed sarcasm and something to eat. That
is why He was friends with men who were handy with fishing nets: He
was always hungry.' Later, you delivered hot chocolate to my window, gave

me extra whipped cream. We talked about His
hands. You asked, 'Is there anything else you need?' 'Only
a two-pound piece for the washing machine.' 'Here, fished from the sofa, by
        my son'.

Danger Bath

As we sat, impeccably dressed, in the Danger Bath,
I told Robbie about the OCD and he talked about the divorce.

There is a rumour that a girl was found naked in here – the
Danger Bath, lockless, waiting. I talked a lot about humiliation

with Robbie, the shame of being seven and unable to divide,
the drive to wash away the laughter with an acceptance letter –

he joked about incontinence at Cornish beaches. In the Danger Bath,
Adam and I shared stories of being sick in awkward places, blocking sinks,

ruining exam scripts. I tried to feed him left-over pizza, and he took
an awfully slow bite, and said, my stomach is so small. The Danger Bath

hears it all. Even the Fellow gets in sometimes, and whispers about
his boarding school. I am glad that he never has to go back.

In the Danger Bath, Mien told me about God, and maybe having TB –
as if we needed any more communicable disease –

but everything was communicable, really.
We were always walking in on one another's truths.

Double Sonnet to Edward Cullen, Dying of Spanish Flu

'In all the chaos of the epidemic, no-one would ever realise I was gone.'
(From Midnight Sun *by Stephenie Meyer)*

These days, handsome young men die quickly.
You were slower than most, though, sweating
through your pyjamas, sweating through your
strange bronze hair. You would have made
a fine corpse somewhere, mud spattered and
gangrenous, but, then, would anyone (apart from
the poets and Ancestry.com) really care
for your beauty? Because what is beauty
when there is no capacity to clean your teeth
or see your fiancée or have warm feet
or feel your face beneath the chin strap
of a helmet, your face beneath the
incandescent bulbs? Your teenage years
were burned up by adults.

What do you do when you are seventeen and the
world is ending? When you are seventeen you are
told that you should take chance on the chin
and live, live, live. Forevers are earnest
and empty and your shoes on the pavement
sound like the shattering heartbeats
of God. Now, all days are spent under duvets,
drifting between fever dreams of holding
someone's hand, or standing at a busy stall of
flowers, or taking a bus. Does it matter that the secret
to living forever is in your doctor's teeth? You just
want a nice day at the beach. You want to swim
in the sea with a nice girl. You want to fall
asleep happy; you want some ice cream.

Mango Leaves

I pin the mango

leaves to the cork
board outside my door.

As they dry, they
wave, the way I

can't. I am ready
to be peeled now.

If only someone could
see my eye, round

as a stone, through
the peephole.

Woodland For Sale

I would work on a development
of fairy rings; loop after loop
of polka-dot, poodle-skirt
toadstools, rehoming the fairies

falling from heads in exam halls.
I'd reintroduce the wolf
to his old friends
and end the practice of pond dipping

in favour of pond diving.
The lakes I would decorate
with the eerie jewellery of frogspawn
and big breasted lily-pads;

the streams I would fill with miniature
belugas and all the tuna I regret eating.
I would seed a few forget-me-nots
next to a swing, which the centaurs

could look upon, but not sit on,
mourning being born, foreign
under their own firmament.
It would rain beetles, spit spiders,

drizzle deer, which would land, unphased,
antlers raised, spun with bone and grace,
trotting on. I'd have unknowable bird song.

I would plant daisies as deeply as tattoos.

I would make kingfishers less camera shy
and find the water voles and mice and
kiss each of their baby heads, one at a time.
I would sprout rabbits in holes

like spring-pricked bulbs, I would
melt dinosaur toys back
to dinosaur oil, give it proper burials.
I'd toil in my woodland

for hours, hoping that somehow
with love, and grubby thumbs,
I could salt the flowers with bees
and give back all the trees.

The Big Tree Across the River

I am the big tree across the river and I am reaching
through your window and into your ear canal.
I am going to whisper sweet nothings about the birds.
They like to perch on the spire of my heart and I have
watched them make love. I like that when the eggs
hatch there is wet delight and viscous squawking.

You wouldn't believe what the people who live
in between us get up to on the weekends.
And the weekdays too. They are loving in a way
you simply cannot imagine. Nice house. Nice garden.
Two children and a dog called Stanley. Never illegal
for them to get married. I am the big tree

across the river and I know everything. Let me
tell you what you think about. Waking up in
a bright aubade with a woman. Touching
her breasts and eating toast. The lights in the room
throbbing. You can pay the rent and save for a
weekend away in Edinburgh. But you're still

hung up on the girl you tongued once in summer term!
What woman would want *you*: a *poet*, a *moper*? Pathetic.

Kiss Me

Yesterday, a dog
barked at me.
On the glass,
his paw
spread like a flower.
He looked at me,
so earnestly,

like a lover.
By the lake,
I wanted something
to crawl out
and kiss me.

Laying in Bed

thinking about my dogs dying.
I'm only awake because I wanted
to watch the sunrise: Self-Care Sunday.

One incipient Saturday mum
placed them on our knees.
They drooled profusely and fell

asleep in the crook of our elbows.
Thinking about digging
a hole in the back corner

of the flower-bed makes me
want to ice-cream scoop
my eyes. Thinking about kissing

the inner silk of those ears while
their little souls leave
makes me want to gargle petrol.

I am glad dogs can only think
like three-year-olds.
Apparently, I was a happy toddler.

Cytoplasm

Blister on my finger grows, the chasm
between bone and the outer ring
of skin, the skin filling with
glassy liquid, the inside
of the plaster like an open
egg and I am queasy
at the sight of my weeping
fingernails, the eager yellow
jelly, all the yolks I haven't
eaten, the whites of someone
else's eyes in the mirror,
the hours I spent revising,
the magic of a callus, how
proud I felt when people
stroked it. There is an echo
of me in the Sellotape
stuck to my walls where
I would hang up the
minutes like little
murderers, where I
would watch the
post-it notes grow
like sores, the formulas
tremulous as I stared.
I swear that they
would bleed in
the night. I
would bleed

in the night
and someone
would comment
on my scooped
out sockets
and say I was as
pale as anything.
Iron deficiency.
Haunting. A
smattering
of ectoplasm,
the poor
lighting,
the shadow
of my
former
self.

small poem

love letter
from me to Siberia

tea bag in water
you samovar

small poem
a thurible

sifting incense
like post

small poem
heart luggage

small poem
for under
your pillow

For Keats

When I make my bed I think
of the women weeping in your
bedrooms, sighing through
those windows – your windows –
the ghost of the cat curling
about their ankles, your auburn
hair in a locket in a cabinet
next door. I wonder how splendid
or normal you looked in
the sun, looked under a candle,
looked out at the plum tree,
the steps, that sky. It's raining,
John, bring a coat. Do you
have the same circle of parched
skin on the pad of your finger
that I do? When I was locked
in a little room I thought
of you relentlessly. The bells
at midnight. The bells
at 1 a.m. Can't you see who it is
weeping in rooms for your
spooled up soul; for your
pent up genius; for your poor fiancée;
for preventable deaths; for death;
for you, John, for you?

Jesus, making a table

Yeshua

     Yeshua

          Yeshua

               through the trees.
Their bare bodies litter your yard, the bark
in reems. You are squaring logs with an adz,

you are sanding. You are thinking of how a stream
makes a ravine. You are sanding. Your father
plastered the walls, built the beams above you,

clapped dusty hands and panelled the sky. The
bowdrill is boring into the soft meat of the cedar,
the sawdust pooling at your feet. What marvellous

feet. Do you remember being a small boy, being dusk-like,
dirty? You would watch the wood become smoother
through hours. You know how to coax something lovely

out of the ringed corpse, the way you tease Olive-Tree
Warblers from men's necks and watch them line
your inner arms. The flat back of the table is laid out

like a gift. Your fingertips are just as unique
as mine. I could not lift a mallet, but you?
There are no unsteady carpenters. A lifetime

of shouldering dead trees, and you are saying to me
Why did you think that my arms were too weak to hold you?

Sad Walk
For Kit

Watching Mars, we slouch the curve
around Selwyn, you rescuing me
from the salmon-coloured hell of the
English faculty, me listening to you
joke about billowing scarves and
handkerchiefs. My shirt is undone
to my bellybutton and the night
rubs my tummy. Your St Paul's school
voice soothes along the gravel path;
we consider jumping the fence
into Caius' playing field, daring
the barbed wire, but I'm
wearing heels and you –
you have never jumped anything.
The sky is a gown and I am lost
in the sleeves. You fit perfectly.
You have taken this Roman road
before, pointing out ancient details
like cabbages. Sad walk. The M11 roaring
just over yonder. In a few weeks, I'll give
up walking for crying, but you can
multitask. Back along the street
we take up everything, loud and
sad as I have ever been till
we reach the playground and s w i n g.
You propel the roundabout
with angst, and Mars watches release
as our feet leave the mud.

An Abundance of Cucumbers

Retirement mornings are spent at the allotment.
He has transplanted dopey sunflowers
from the garden, and the shed dries garlic
in large white fists, like those that grip the spade
and de-bramble the hazel tree – sharp labour
but worth it come winter. We have an abundance of cucumbers

– I don't like them but fork them in anyway. Cucumbers
till the end of days, at which point the allotment
can supply us with root vegetables and labour
and something for my art – sunflowers
over and over. I'll catch my reflection in a spade
and perfume myself with a crush of garlic.

Dad has stopped asking me to turn the beds. My love of garlic
is not the same as having a tenderness for cucumbers
or the strength or will or to hoist and hold a spade.
Even what I can offer falls short. I'm no Heaney. The allotment
looks vague and flat in my phrases and I can't get the sunflowers
quite right. Too bright. Too round and winking. Not enough labour

to stretch myself with. My body has one job. The labour
of sestinas can't be enough, can it? Dad cracks a garlic
head and dices finely. I'm still trying to trap sunflowers
in a complicated house with many rooms. Locals collect cucumbers
from our front door. The allotment
has been beset by blight and the spade

lifts out survivors. I look for my poems among the tomatoes but the spade
shakes its gunmetal head. It will be a labour
to replant but it must be done. Dad must have the allotment
so he can grow again. The garlic
is like the segmented, bloody body of an orange and the cucumbers
reach a crescendo. The sunflowers

leer over my shoulder. The sunflowers
are already parents. Can you cut off a ram's head with a spade?
I'm in a wheelbarrow surrounded by cucumbers.
I am the colour of a sunset. I am haunted by the labour
of hollowing out a pumpkin. Which one of you is the garlic?
Who wears the wading boots? At the allotment

I am skinning cucumbers, trying to halve our labour.
Dad loves sunflowers but they do nothing. The spade
a speculum. An organ of garlic erupts in the next allotment.

To Beatrice, on Castle Mound

Now that I am free, you promise me anything I want.
So, we climb through the pure, excavating air, to sit close.
How are you not freezing? – your sheer, fairy dress fluttering, the haunt
of your hair. You talk about your soft, uptilting nose,
and I am looking at your cobbled freckles
and you let me touch your fluffed split ends.
The fens are out there, filled with deer. Up here, my blood gales
with longing. You let me wear your girlfriend's brother's cardigan and
I am thinking of writing on your tracing paper collarbone, but I don't say so.
Not because you don't know, but because you'd enjoy me admitting
too much. You scoff at my poems
and then quote them to me. You lean in for a kiss
and blow it to the moon, saying how pretty she is.
I touch your knee. You tell me to write this.

When the Hoover Sucked Up My Crucifix

I laughed and laughed. Kevin and I,
gloved, masked, heard it rattle

through the tubing: ascending. Imagine
us unscrewing the head of the hoover

to look for the body of God.
Imagine us scooping out uni

dust on to the floor, detangling
our housemates' hair and sifting

sixty years' worth of student skin
through our fingers to find Christ.

Imagine us trapped together, just ten
days ago: strangers. Imagine Kevin

on his hands and knees, palms filled
with couscous, two-pence pieces

and absurdity; me: coughing periodically.
Imagine us hooking the Cross

from a thick layer of bottle tops,
beaming miraculously.

For Peter

You have but a few glasses.
Their lips are dusty, the sofa's
musty, the green velvet was plush,
once. The two lightbulbs are
clinical, not nearly Edwardian
enough for your tastes, and you talk
of having them replaced
with those nice chandeliers.
For now, we must make do
with the lampshade made
from what seems to be the Dean's
wife's old nightdress, and stem
with the effect of a candle melting.
The real thing, you say bitterly,
would be a fire risk. Peter,
the real thing is in your books
of Latin; the Roman wine
that you specialise in;
the windows which rattle
their antiquity, the genuine
pew inexplicably in your room;
the way you talk of marine
archaeology; the way I listen.

Stephen the Phlebotomist

How bored you are, explaining phenotypes to me.
I stammer about GCSE biology; I have forgotten T cells exist,
I have forgotten clots, platelets, osmotic pressure,

I have forgotten my birthday. You hand me another form;
like mine, your hands are small. I wonder how many times
a day you ask which arm, how many times across your life

you will request a rolled up sleeve. 'Left,' I say.
The lilac tourniquet clasps my tattoo and you remove
your gloves to seek a vein. Some days, my skin is suffocating.

Some days, it is remote. But here, the eye of the needle blinking,
you: talking, me: bleeding, I feel something like normalcy.
Because haven't humans always done this? Opened our veins

to each other, watched faith trickle from the crook
of our elbows: hoping, hoping for better? You say
the way we treat the vulnerable says it all. The vials

are filling with such constancy that for the first time
in my life I love my heart. Stephen, I have never been sanguine.
But for you I split a smile and say 'My friend Em wants some.

My blood, that is.' You call her a freak, which is fair.
O Stephen – I have forgotten how to be empty.
I have forgotten how to be scared.

Algebra

Little rat claws pitter-patter. Cause paper
cuts up the muscled wall of a heart. Orange juice
fills pockets, pockets lined with shards of shredded tissue
breeding ardently, breeding beyond number –
it's an afterbirth; it's the mess
I'll use to replaster the ceiling. Scratch

at the skirtings first thing every morning. I scratch
like a street cat in summer. Got that paper
back and keened at the floodlights – the mess
I'd made of the twelve-marker! The answer was *The juice
of love is nectareous and desperate*; I wrote *The number
on the sheet's a seamy lust.* Spent a tissue

burnishing a ballpoint hickey, a tissue
cleaning up the climax of an essay. There's a scratch
on my retina, I can't see my candidate number
but it pulses hotly on the paper,
bald and flush and glistening. In the hall, they have banned juice
and empathy so I pour mine down the chief invigilator's blouse, make a mess

so big my uniform is used to mop it up. The mess
of the paperwork afterwards. The nurse gives me a tissue
but tells me that I'll have to pay for it. I juice
my hands. Make love to the leg of my desk. Scratch
my scalp nude in the library. Leave paper
about me like used plates at a wake, number

the remaining reasons why my partner loves me, number
them on one terrible hand. Jesus, mum scolds the mess.
I tidy by throwing mugs from my window like paper
planes, lance pedestrians like boils. My last tissue
is a beautiful woman drowned in a lake. White dress, the rest – No. Scratch
that. This. I want a glass of the juice

of human kindness and I want to give it to myself, the juice
and honey I was meant to have. Just a number
on a piece of paper. Just the years of wanting to scratch
a kidney out and sell it to get my head to stop. I'll mess
up the future soon, making canon fodder of the tissues;
I must make this fervid love mean something. I'm going to paper

myself over and – *Scratch my back and I'll* – *Mess*
this up and I'll – I've given you a casket of gin and juice, a cute little number
to wear everywhere. I'm the wasp in the fig's tissue, sharp as a slice of paper.

Annotations

In my mum's copy
of *High Windows*,

she's added
something extra.

Just for me.

Lyric

When I am drying my sheets, I catch a glimpse
of your hair, and have one of Dante Rosetti's

wet dreams. I sleep naked, but wake each morning
clothed in the evening in which we did nothing but kiss.

When I water the strawberry plants, I realise that
Radiohead was right. Your skin makes me cry.

I have taken up Romanian deadlifting so that each
night, your calluses can catch my thighs.

When my professor asks me what I think a lesbian
lyric should be, the page is your name, over and over.

I cup a peach and twist it open. I want
to have you in the park while the ducks watch.

The Finer Details

While trying to build
a koi pond for his wife,
a local man came upon
an unexploded bomb.

His spade must have met
the hard conch
of its tail-cone,
the clanging causing
bells in his head –
precious Roman jewellery?
The Sutton Hoo
of Hertfordshire?
Excalibur? Maybe!
He sifted the earth
with nervous fingers,
thinking of riches
and BBC news crews.

The feline body
of the bomb began
to emerge.

The dirt he piled neatly
by the geraniums, and
the locking-pin he left
in the fuse, unable
to find the wrench
in his shed. He asked
his wife for a glass
of lemonade.

It remains a
mystery how he
managed to drag
the bomb to his car

and drive it to the local
police station.

Once the primary school
and old peoples' home
had been evacuated,
the cops called
the bomb squad,
and we heard their
successful job
ricocheting through
our cupboards and mugs
of tea.

The local man has since
disappeared into urban
myth. Many have tried
to psychoanalyse him.
It has been suggested
that he was trying to drive
the bomb away from his
wife. Or his house. It has
been suggested that he
was an undercover spy,
accidently discovering
a gift. It has been
suggested that he was just
deeply stupid.
But it's the finer details

that interest me. Did he
strap the bomb in?

Did he listen to the radio
as he drove five hundred
pounds of explosives
down the High Road?

Was he thinking of how
far humans have come
from turning sticks and
stones into spears? Was he
thinking of the choices
made by men decades ago?
Guessing is hopeless.

But I like to believe,

as he loaded the device
into the back of his Nissan
Micra, and let it breathe on
him,

that he was simply
creating
an elaborate metaphor for
love.

Acknowledgments

Epoque Press – *Epithalamion*
Tower Poetry Competition, Christ Church College, Oxford – *Woodland for Sale*
The Young Poets Network – *Cytoplasm, Stephen the Phlebotomist, Double Sonnet to Edward Cullen, Dying of Spanish Flu*
The Mays Anthology – *small poem*
Cambridge University Poetry and Prose Society – *Sad Walk*
perhappened – *When the Hoover Sucked Up my Crucifix*

Lightning Source UK Ltd.
Milton Keynes UK
UKHW010918280622
405068UK00002B/108